Martin Luther

Hero of Faith

By Edward C. Grube

Illustrated by Deborah J. White

D1528479

CONCORDIA PUBLISHING HOUSE • SAINT LOUIS

Copyright © 2012 Concordia Publishing House
3558 S. Jefferson Ave., St. Louis, MO 63118-3968
1-800-325-3040 · www.cph.org

Written by Edward C. Grube
Illustrated by Deborah J. White
Edited by Rodney L. Rathmann
Editorial assistant: Amanda G. Lansche

Manufactured in East Peoria, IL / 63692 / 160152

Table of Contents

Martin Luther

foreword

The life and work of Martin Luther is well documented and well speculated. Separation of fact from popular legend is the work of Luther scholars, and we gratefully acknowledge their efforts.

This biography borrows from the concept that created Table Talk, a collection of casual but significant conversations that occurred around Luther's dinner table. In creating *Lunch with Luther*, the author begs indulgence (forgive me!) as he places Dr. Luther as a guest at a Lutheran school lunch table. Fiction creeps into the scenarios, but only as a device to contextualize Luther's wisdom. These pages portray Luther as a person who would interact with people today, just as he did in his Table Talk experiences. The biography is not chronological, but instead reflects a random scattering of questions and conversation that might guide the conversation among Luther and several students.

You will read the words of a narrator—an imaginary student who guides the discourse—

along with questions and comments of other imaginary children. Special thanks go to Renee Grube and her students at Concord Lutheran School in Bensenville, Illinois, who helped me to think like a student in Luther's company.

A foreword for students appears in the opening paragraphs of the biography.

Edward C. Grube

hero of
faith

95 THESES

The World of Martin Luther

Older students like you aren't often asked to use your imagination. But if you can dream a little, it may help you understand the world-class genius Martin Luther. Many books tell about Luther's work, and authors have written fine biographies of his life. You may even want to read one or more of them after you meet Dr. Luther.

Yes, imagine you are meeting Martin Luther in person. He decided to visit your school. Would you invite him to eat lunch with you? You might be relieved that he isn't visiting religion class or sitting next to you in chapel. You might expect him to want to hear you confess a flawless Apostles' Creed or to sing one of his famous hymns from memory! But, he just wants to talk. He wants you to ask questions. He wants to share his knowledge, his stories, his humor, and most of all, his faith. Some of his best teaching happened around a crowded dinner table.

By the way, sometimes you'll hear Luther mix in a German word or two as he speaks. Oh, and what should you call him? It is proper to address him as Dr. Luther, because his university studies earned him the right to be called *doctor*, as you might call a teacher at a college today. You can call him *reverend* or *pastor* too. Not only did he teach about the Bible, but he also was pastor of a church.

Well, let's get back to you and Luther and lunch. Imagine that Luther takes you aside and quietly asks about the lunch menu. "You don't suppose, *mein Freund,* that your cooks have prepared some sausages and crusty rye bread, do you?"

You might be happy that he called you his friend, and you certainly don't want to disappoint such an important and friendly guest. What can you offer that might even come close to his beloved sausages and rye bread? Maybe he could learn to like hot dogs on a bun.

As you lead Luther to your table, you ask, "What food did you enjoy when you were young?"

Maybe Luther could learn to like hot dogs on a bun.

"My family began with very little. My parents were careful and tried to save. We moved when I was about one year old so my father could buy a copper mine and earn a better living. It's hard to remember way back then, but families like ours often ate cheap pork along with dark bread and turnips.

Sometimes we ate porridge, a thick soup made of oats boiled in water. Not exactly hot dogs on a bun, *ja*? But you know what I really remember about our family meals? I remember my brother Jacob sitting next to me. Ah, dear Jacob loved me, and I loved him. Don't you think that meals with people you love are always good meals?

"Oh, but you asked about food. As my father began to make more money, our food improved. Germany had fine fields for growing grains to make bread, and there were pastures for raising cattle. Only the nobles in their castles had what you would call fine dining. Yet, God provided the food we needed. I didn't really enjoy food until Katie and I were married.

"We did not have refrigerators, so much of what we ate was smoked, pickled, or salted. *Ach du lieber!* I mean, oh, my dear! Salted herring! I fondly remember the first time I met Katie. You know, she had quite an adventure with fish barrels. *Jawohl!* She and some other nuns escaped from a convent. They hid in a wagon transporting fish barrels, from which salted herring was sold! Can you imagine that?

"The meals I remember best were during the days that Katie, our children, many guests, and I lived in a building called the Black Cloister, in Wittenberg, Germany, a small town on the Elbe River. The cloister

My visit with you reminds me of those days.

was a wedding gift to us. We partied! Katie always
made enough to eat, even though we never knew
how many students from my university would show
up. Some even lived with us. Besides the students,

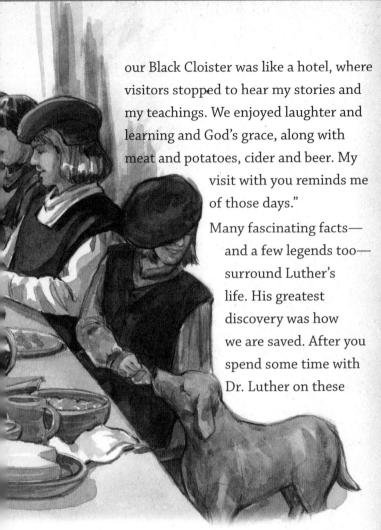

our Black Cloister was like a hotel, where visitors stopped to hear my stories and my teachings. We enjoyed laughter and learning and God's grace, along with meat and potatoes, cider and beer. My visit with you reminds me of those days."

Many fascinating facts—and a few legends too—surround Luther's life. His greatest discovery was how we are saved. After you spend some time with Dr. Luther on these pages, you might want to read *Luther: Biography of a Reformer* by Frederick Nohl—but not during lunch!

We will do lunch again tomorrow. Luther will be pleased to answer your questions. Invite your friends!

◆ ◆ ◆

day two

A Reformation

Can you imagine Dr. Luther's surprise when the cooks prepared a special menu? Sit down and enjoy a heaping helping of sauerkraut, knockwurst, and rye bread. If Luther says something like *wunderbar*, you'll know he thinks the food is wonderful.

Maybe today's lunch would be a good time to ask Luther about his childhood, his home, and what school was like. What are you waiting for? *Macht schnell!* (If you're not quick enough, he might go sit with someone who will ask silly questions such as "What kind of computer did you use to distribute your famous Theses?" Or maybe you were wondering that yourself.)

Luther posts his famous theses—all ninety-five of them.

You decide to talk about his childhood later. Maybe over dessert. Maybe the cooks will make apple strudel! Oh, it's so easy to be sidetracked by food!

"Dr. Luther, how did you think of the Eighty-five Theses?"

"The actual number was ninety-five. But more important, do you know what *theses* are?"

Well, you didn't want to admit it, but with all this talk in Lutheran schools about Luther's Ninety-five Theses, you didn't want others to laugh if you didn't know what *theses* are, much less so many of them.

Luther adds, "I guess if you find it hard to remember the number of theses, you can't be blamed if you don't know what they are. Hmmm. I'll trade you my answer for half of that peanut butter and jelly sandwich. I've never tasted one of those."

Just as you offer Luther half of your sandwich, he laughs and says, "No, no, *mein Freund*, I was just joking. You see, I often suffer with a sick stomach. I probably should not try anything new."

Secretly, you wonder how a stomach stuffed with sauerkraut and sausage would have trouble with a PB&J. But you don't ask. Instead, you remind your famous friend that he was explaining *Theses*—all ninety-five of them. (It was ninety-five, wasn't it?)

Dr. Luther munches his rye bread and continues. "*Theses* are ideas, done after much study, that try to explain a belief or viewpoint. My theses were an open invitation to discuss serious errors in what the Roman Catholic Church taught. You see, Pope Leo X and the Roman Catholic Church slipped away from the Bible's teachings and taught other things instead. I found ninety-five points that I wanted the pope and other leaders to consider. I wanted to show them how they went wrong. I wanted to debate them, so they would start teaching the truth again."

Pope Leo X and other leaders were very angry with what Martin Luther wrote and said.

I asked, "How did they feel about your ideas? I heard that Pope X wasn't too happy with them."

"Pope who?"

"Pope X."

"Don't feel hurt, *mein Freund*, if I laugh. *Leo* was the pope's name. The X is a Roman numeral. He was known as Pope Leo the Tenth. Pope Leo and other leaders were very angry with what I wrote and said. They refused to believe me. Worse than that, they refused to believe the Bible."

"Okay, so now I know what *theses* are. I don't think I want to hear all of them, but could you tell me a few?"

"Lunch would not be long enough to talk about all ninety-five, and the vocabulary is pretty much what you would hear in college. So let me tell you about some of the teachings that my Ninety-five Theses argued against.

"How would you like to be told that you should purchase some certificates, called *indulgences*, that would pay for some of your sins? How would you like to be taught—oh, your good Lutheran school teachers would shudder—that when you die, you wouldn't go to heaven? Instead, you would go to a place called *purgatory*—somewhere between hell and heaven— until you suffered for your sins?

"That would frighten you. It might frighten you and your family enough to fall for a special fund-raiser, where dollars could buy time that you would otherwise spend in purgatory.

"A man named Johann Tetzel was quite successful with this fund-raiser. Poor people

Johann Tetzel was quite successful with this fund-raiser.

paid lots of money to buy their dead loved ones less time in purgatory. My theses pointed out ninety-five ways that this was wrong. However, since loss of sales meant less money for Pope Leo X and the other Church leaders of the day, you can imagine why those leaders wanted to kill me. I thought of this as a reformation; they thought of it as a revolution."

You ask, "Why was this so important to you?"

Almost choking on a chunk of sausage, Luther, sounding sad and a bit angry at the same time, answers, "Why was this so important to me? It was important because of you and millions of people like you." Luther's voice softened. "Do you believe that Jesus loves you? Do you know that Jesus suffered, died, was buried, and rose from the dead to take away your sins? Do you believe that Jesus did everything needed to pay for your sins? Do you know that you can't do anything—not all the most wonderful things in the world—to help pay for your sins? Do you know that you don't have to? Jesus' gift of eternal life in heaven is free! It's a gift."

Whew. You thought *you* were supposed to ask the questions! You have to admit, though, that you could answer *yes* to all of Luther's questions.

Then you realize what just happened. Luther didn't post the Ninety-five Theses because he wanted to start trouble or have schools and churches named after him. He discovered unbiblical teachings that threatened the faith of frightened sinners. His arguments were more than history. The Holy Spirit used Luther's courage and his Bible study so your Lutheran school could teach how Jesus really saved you. What more can you say?

"Thank You, dear God, for sending *mein Freund* to fight the wrong teachings of some very powerful people. And thank you, Dr. Luther, for the Ninety-five Theses. Yes, yes, I remembered this time. **Ninety-five**!" 95 !

"I can hardly wait to hear more about your adventures. But I would like to know a little more about you before we lunch together again. When is your birthday?"

"I was born on November 10, 1483," Luther replies. "My father's name was Hans, and my mother's name was Margarethe. My Baptism date is even more important. My parents took me to be baptized on November 11. They knew the importance of Baptism! I'll tell you more about my childhood tomorrow."

◆ ◆ ◆
day three
Luther's Early Years

By the end of lunch today, we'll know a whole lot more about Martin Luther. Here he comes now. "Not another knockwurst on rye, Dr. Luther!" you exclaim at the sight of his lunch tray.

"*Ja, ja, ja*. I could eat this every day."

"You promised to tell us about growing up."

"It wasn't always easy, but our home life was typical. Children were often treated more firmly than they are today. Of course, just like you, children were taught to respect their parents and also to fear them. No laws protected children from abuse, and parents often harshly punished their children. My mother and father were very strict, and they did not hesitate to punish me.

"My father hoped I could get a good government job someday so I wouldn't have to work as hard as he did. He wanted me to be an important person. When I was seven, my parents sent me to the Latin school in the city of Mansfeld. Next, I attended a school in the city of Magdeburg. I was fourteen years old. A year later, I went to a school in the city of Eisenach. I lived at the schools."

In fifteenth-century Germany, schools weren't concerned about making learning fun.

"Wow, Dr. Luther. Was going to those schools fun?"

"In fifteenth-century Germany, schools weren't concerned about making learning fun. We students were there to study hard. Our parents expected us not to waste their tuition money. I was an eager learner, and we students found ways to have fun."

I asked, "What did you want to be when you grew up? Did you want to be a pastor? Did you want to reform the Roman Catholic Church?"

"*Nein, mein Freund.* I mean no. My father wanted me to be a lawyer. Working as a lawyer or a pastor were the only important jobs. I decided, with lots of 'help' from my father, to be a lawyer. That way, I could make money to support my family."

"Dr. Luther, did you have to study hard in college?"

"I worked hard, yes, but I was a good student. Learning wasn't difficult for me. I went to the University of Erfurt in 1501, and the next year I earned a bachelor of arts degree. I stayed at the university to earn my master of arts degree, which I was awarded in 1505.

"I stayed in school even longer! I enrolled in law school. My father was very happy. He would be proud to have a successful son—and an obedient one. After all, I was studying to be what he wanted me to be. Yet, I had a strange feeling inside. As good a law student as I was, I couldn't forget some things that happened during the years I had worked on my master of arts degree."

Benny asked, "Oh, Dr. Luther, that sounds serious. What happened? Did you break up with your girlfriend or something?"

Luther laughed so hard that I feared he would choke on his knockwurst!

"No," he gasped. "Life at the university left no time for girlfriends. Besides, girls were not welcome at universities in those days. No, I just had many things to think about. I really don't like to talk about them."

Not wanting to make Dr. Luther uncomfortable, but also curious about his past, I introduced him to more friends who joined us for lunch. They were on the Saturday bowling team and had heard a rumor that Luther was a bowler. While they talked, I went to the computer lab for some quick research.

I couldn't find much about the mysterious experiences that Luther didn't want to talk about. Some researchers think that he suffered some kind of accident that almost cost him his life. They also thought the death of a friend deeply troubled him. Religion began to bother him too. He wondered many things about God. Okay, because even experts weren't sure about things on which Luther was quiet, I decided to give up on my line of questions.

Getting back to the lunch table, I wondered what I missed. Everyone was laughing. It was somewhat messy too, because a laughing Luther was trying to teach the table to say *platzbahnkegln*.

That was the German word for bowling in the 1500s, and it's hard to pronounce without spitting a few crumbs around! Luther explained, "Bowling wasn't an exact sport back then. Some bowlers used three pins; others used as many as seventeen. Made it hard to keep score! I decided that bowling should have nine pins! Many bowlers agreed with that number for three hundred years!"

I was happy that Luther had some enjoyment. I always thought of him reading stacks of books and writing report after report. But I was curious again.

"Dr. Luther, so far it sounds like you would end up as a lawyer, not a pastor or teacher."

"I believe I would have been a successful lawyer too, had it not been for that thunderstorm."

At the mention of "thunderstorm," Alana shrieked! She interrupted, "What were you thinking, being outside in a thunderstorm? You are so smart, and that was so . . ." Alana slapped her hand over her mouth before she finished the sentence. This was *the* Dr. Martin Luther, and she did not want to disrespect him.

This must have been the day for Luther to laugh a lot, for now he was laughing with Alana.

He said, "Yes, yes, it seems that Alana knows some of my history. She has heard the story of my decision to become a church worker—a monk, to be exact—a student of religion known as a *theologian*. You'll like this story—unless you're afraid of thunderstorms! The story goes that I had had a few days of vacation at home, and I was returning to the university. I couldn't walk fast enough to stay ahead of an approaching storm. One bolt of lightning struck very close to me. Its energy knocked me to the ground."

I asked, "What does that have to do with becoming a monk?"

"Oh, I had been thinking about God and all kinds of religious questions for many years. When I went to school to study law, I could have studied religion instead—theology, to be more exact. But, as you know, my father wanted a lawyer in the family. Now, back to the lightning.

"Have you ever been close to a lightning strike? I was more frightened than I thought possible. In a flash, I thought of St. Anne, who was the patron saint of miners. I remember learning about her in school. So I screamed, 'Help, St. Anne, and I'll become a monk!'

Help, St. Anne, and I'll become a monk!

"As soon as the shock wore off, I was sorry I had made that promise to St. Anne. I am, however, a man of my word. I became a dropout so I could become a monk. Father was not happy when I joined the Reformed Congregation of the Eremitical Order of St. Augustine in Erfurt, Germany.

"Perhaps we should talk more about that tomorrow. That's where my life gets really interesting—when God led me to help His people for generations to come. Besides, I'd like to try rolling some ten pins. Can't be too much harder than nine!"

A Time of Struggle

Guess what Dr. Luther has for lunch today. If you're thinking sausage on rye, you're wrong. He has Italian beef on a roll. Since he plans to talk about the pope today, he said he might as well eat a sandwich with Italian origins. The Vatican, where the pope lives and rules, is located inside Rome, Italy. Though Luther likes the sandwich, Rome holds many bad memories for him. We'll get to those memories later.

We finished yesterday's conversation hearing that Luther promised to become a monk. Still, one would not have blamed him for changing his mind, because he made his decision under a lot of stress.

"Dr. Luther, what happened after you became a monk?"

"Becoming a monk was hard. I worked long hours studying to become a priest. I did well. I entered the monastery in 1505, and I became a priest in 1507. Oh, but my heart was troubled all during this time. I had lots of questions about whether or not I was saved."

Logan said, "You can't be serious, Dr. Luther. All of us in our Lutheran school know how Jesus saved us. With all your studies, I can't believe we know more than you knew!"

"Think about what you're saying, *mein Freund*," said Dr. Luther. "How is it that you know what Jesus did for you? How is it that you know you are saved

I was trying to earn God's favor without accepting what Jesus did for me. I felt doomed.

as a gift from God? How do you know that you can-not and need not do anything to save yourself from your sins and go to heaven?"

"Oooh. I guess I offended you, Dr. Luther. I'm sorry," said Logan.

"Ah, forgiveness is yours. After all, that's what Jesus gives to all of us. I learned that good news only after punishing myself for thinking that I had to earn God's love. I tortured myself with hard labor and agonized praying—all in an attempt to please God. I was trying to earn God's favor without accepting what Jesus did for me. I felt doomed."

It didn't take me long to become a teacher at the University of Wittenberg.

"And—forgive me if I whisper—I even hated God because of what I thought He demanded of me.

"Some of my teachers worried about me. I was depressed. I was desperate. One of my teachers, Johann von Staupitz, decided I would get my mind off my worries if I spent even more time in school."

"Hey, Dr. Luther, that's exactly what my mom tells me!" said Benny from the end of the table. "She says, 'Benny, stop worrying about basketball, football, and Ping-Pong. Pay attention to your studies in school, or you might be there a long, long, long time.'"

Luther smiled. "Oh, Benny, thanks for understanding. You know, I studied hard, and what I learned—or what I didn't learn—was hard on me. I went to advanced theology school at the University of Erfurt. It didn't take me long to become a teacher at the University of Wittenberg. I also took courses while I taught. I earned a doctor of theology degree."

"Dr. Luther, did you use all your education to teach in a Lutheran school?" It was Benny again. Benny brought another smile to Dr. Luther's face.

"No, Benny. There were no Lutheran schools. The Roman Catholics were in charge of many schools. The head of the Catholic Church—the pope—was like a king. He expected all the leaders of all the regions and all the teachers in all the schools to obey him and believe what he told them to believe."

"Kind of sounds like some of our teachers," Benny began, but Luther motioned him to be quiet.

"No, no, Benny. To disagree with the pope was dangerous in ways that could cost you your life. It's not at all like being grounded because you forgot your memory work. Now, what was I saying? Oh, I remember. Listen carefully.

"The more I learned about what the Church of my day was teaching, and the more I studied, the more I didn't understand. I found no comfort in my knowledge of Jesus. I was terrified of God. I understood that God knew all about me, and because of that, I certainly didn't think He would want me in heaven!"

Pedro had a question. "Dr. Luther, do you think God abandoned you? Did He leave you on your own?"

"I certainly felt that way. I wanted answers to my question of how I was to be saved. I studied and studied. I didn't understand that this was the way

God decided to be with me. He drove me to learn what I would need to know later. You see, I had to debate and defend God's Word with brilliant and respected teachers—teachers who taught the wrong things about God's Word."

I wanted answers to my question of how I was to be saved.

"I studied as God led me to study. Though I did not find peace and happiness as I learned what others had to say about the Bible's truth, I learned enough to lecture many students and to become an expert on the Psalms and the Books of Romans, Galatians, and Hebrews. I even worked my way up to being in charge of eleven monasteries."

"And that didn't make you happy?" I asked.

"I could never be happy until I knew I was saved."

"Do you think the devil was working on you?"

"*Jawohl!* A thousand times, yes! Satan can turn God's Word upside down and convince weak believers—even very educated believers—of lies. Satan never gives up. Even after I learned the truth of how I was saved, Satan tormented me. I had to tell him over and over to get away from me."

"Uh, you talked to the devil, Dr. Luther?" asked Angelica, rolling her eyes.

"Sure. Don't you? You have to drive him away every day."

"Is that what you meant when you wrote about 'daily drowning the old Adam'?"

"*Jawohl*, again!"

Benny jumped in. "I'll go get some water!"

"Benny, Benny. Are you baptized?"

"Yes, but I don't remember it. Maybe I need it again."

"You must study my catechism better, Benny. One thing I learned and taught from my studies was that you don't have to have a memory that extends back to the day you were baptized. However, you should know what happened when you were baptized."

"Oh, I know that. Jesus took away my sins, and the Holy Spirit gave me faith to believe that Jesus is my Savior. Did you learn that when you got your doctor of theology degree?"

Now it was my turn to motion Benny to be quiet. But Dr. Luther saw me.

"It is okay for Benny to ask questions about God and the Bible and his faith. That's exactly what needs to happen in your school. Those questions give your teachers a chance to teach what they learned from the Bible. Those questions are ways that the Holy Spirit strengthens your faith.

"I have only one more day with you. Tomorrow, if you're interested, I'll tell you the scariest part of my story."

"Does it have a happy ending, Dr. Luther?" asked Benny.

"You attend a Lutheran school, which has taught you the truth about Jesus, Benny. Do you think it has a happy ending?"

"*Jawohl!*" Benny said, laughing.

Now everybody smiled!

Of Grace and Truth

"Hi, Dr. Luther. Today is your last lunch with us. But we have so many questions left!"

"Yeah," said Benny. "I'd like to know why you didn't bring your kids to lunch. Maybe they could have taught us some German games."

"Yes, they would have enjoyed that. We had a big family. Katie and I had six children—Hans, Elisabeth, Magdalene,

Katie and I had six children—Hans, Elisabeth, Magdalene, Martin, Paul, and Margarethe.

Martin, Paul, and Margarethe. I don't think I was ever so sad as when our baby Elisabeth died and later when our darling Magdalene died."

Benny sniffed a little and apologized for asking. But Luther said, "We have great comfort in knowing that Jesus loved Elisabeth and Magdalene. They, too, had the gift of salvation and the gift of faith."

"I'm thinking you must have been even happier about your discoveries when they died."

"Yes, but my 'discoveries' caused terrible arguments, and my own Church thought I was a heretic."

Benny opened his mouth to ask a question, but before he could say anything, Luther said, "A *heretic* is someone who teaches lies about God and the Bible."

"But you taught the truth," blurted Benny.

"I did," agreed Luther. "Do you want to hear that story?"

We all gave Luther our full attention. This was to be an account about an adventure with a happy ending.

"This happened before I married Katie and had a family. I'm glad it happened then; otherwise, their lives would have been in danger just like mine.

"I was a very serious student of the Bible. One day, I came across this passage in Paul's Letter to the Romans: 'All have sinned and fall short of the glory of God, and are justified by His grace as a gift, through the redemption that is in Christ Jesus' (Romans 3:23–24).

"My Church and many of its leaders did not tell the truth. I pointed out their mistakes by using the Bible. They taught that you had to earn or pay for God's forgiveness. When I read more of Paul's letters, I can hardly tell you how happy I was! You don't have to pay for your own sins with good works or money. Jesus saved you by grace alone, the purest of love. Then, by the Holy Spirit's power in Baptism and the Bible, He gives us faith to believe in this gift.

I can hardly tell you how happy I was!

"I was happy to know the truth, but the pope in Rome and many leaders in the government were angry. They didn't want to believe the Bible. They continued to teach things not found in God's Word. I was especially upset with Johann Tetzel. He was fooling people into thinking they could buy their way into heaven. That was the Ninety-three Theses incident."

"Ninety-five," Benny corrected.

"Ah! I was just testing to see if you were listening, Benny," Luther laughed.

"I continued to teach that we are saved by God's grace through faith alone, even when the Church and government leaders told me to stop. I was in trouble with the pope, who wanted to throw me out of the Church. They call it *excommunication*. I had to defend myself. Emperor Charles the Fifth put me on trial in the city of Worms. He had a legal responsibility over German universities and professors. These obstacles to the Gospel were giving me a chance to say I was wrong about my teachings— or to insist that I was right."

"Were you afraid? Were you tempted to say you were wrong?" asked Frederic.

"I thought about all the things I taught and all the things they taught. I wanted to be right. The truth about salvation was on trial more than I was. Oh, but I prayed! I wanted to be sure I was following God's Word and not just my own thoughts. Finally, I was ready to answer.

"I don't know that I remember the exact words, but I said something like this: 'Unless I am convinced by proofs from Scripture or by clear reasoning that Scripture leads me to, I cannot and will not retract, for it is neither safe nor wise to do anything against conscience. God help me. Amen.'"

"Great answer!" blurted Benny.

These obstacles to the Gospel were giving me a chance to say I was wrong about my teachings—or to insist that I was right.

Luther said, "They didn't think so. The emperor said I was an outlaw. I was to be arrested. It was against the law to read what I had written. Men were free to kill me. No one was supposed to help me."

"Didn't you have any friends?" asked Frederic.

"Yes, God gave me brave friends. Several princes in Germany decided to help me, but they didn't let me in on their plans! Oh, was I frightened when they 'kidnapped' me on my way home from Worms! Prince Frederick the Wise, my supporter, arranged this kidnapping and whisked me away into hiding. He hid me in the Wartburg castle in Eisenach, Germany. I was safe, but I really wasn't free to go anywhere."

"Were you lonely, Dr. Luther?" I asked.

"I didn't have much time to be lonely. I wanted to do one important thing for the German people. They could not read the Bible for themselves because it wasn't written in German. I spent my time translating the Bible so they could read God's truth for themselves. Ah, and write, write, write—I had so much to teach about God's truth because lies had been taught for so very long.

"I also read and answered letters that my best friend, Philip Melanchthon, and others wrote to ask for advice and what I had learned in all my studies of God's Word."

Prince Frederick hid me in the Wartburg castle in Eisenach, Germany. I was safe, but I really wasn't free to go anywhere.

"How long did you have to stay in that cold, damp castle? Did it have creaky doors and candles covered in cobwebs?" asked Benny.

I think Luther giggled. He said, "I was there about a year. I just couldn't stay much longer. I felt I had to get back to the church I had served. I worried that the people might be misled without me. So, I left and began preaching in Wittenberg. I taught and preached and wrote. And, as you already know, I married Katie—a runaway nun from a convent! Oh, she was wonderful.

Thanks for joining me for lunch.
Auf Wiedersehen, alle meine Freunde!

I loved her so much. If you read more about me, be sure to read about her too.

"I must go now. I'm glad you attend a Lutheran school. But, you know, I really didn't want schools or churches to be named after me. I am glad you can read God's Word in your own language. In God's Word, everyone can find the peace and joy I have in knowing Jesus as my Savior and the forgiveness and salvation that are ours in Him. These are His gifts to us—gifts we receive from Him by faith alone. Thanks for joining me for lunch. *Auf Wiedersehen, alle meine Freunde!*"

Timeline of Events
during Martin Luther's life

1483   Martin Luther born in Eisleben
(November 10)

1498   Luther attends St. George's Church
School in Eisenach

1501   Luther graduates from high school;
enters University of Erfurt

1502   Luther earns bachelor of arts degree

1505   Luther enters Augustinian
monastery at Erfurt

1506   Christopher Columbus dies

1507   Luther is ordained a priest

1508   Luther begins teaching at University
of Wittenberg; Michelangelo begins
painting the Sistine Chapel in Rome

1510–11   Luther visits Rome

1512   Luther receives doctoral degree
in theology

1513   Ponce de Leon discovers Florida;
Balboa sees the Pacific Ocean

1515   Katharina von Bora takes vows
as a nun

1517   Luther posts the Ninety-five Theses
on the door of the Wittenberg Castle
Church

1518   Officials in Rome begin formal
inquiry into Luther's teachings

1519   Magellan begins voyage
to circumnavigate the globe

1520   Luther is threatened with
excommunication from the Roman
Catholic Church; Luther burns the
pope's order to recant

1521   Luther is excommunicated; Luther
ordered to Worms to appear before
the emperor; death sentence
imposed; Luther is kidnapped by
friends and hidden in the Wartburg
castle

1522   Luther returns to Wittenberg

1523	Sister Katharina von Bora and eleven other nuns write Dr. Luther to ask for help in escaping
1525	Katharina (age 26) marries Luther (age 41); they make their home in Wittenberg
1526	Luther's first son, Hans, born
1527	Luther's first daughter, Elisabeth, born; dies five months later
1529	Luther writes the Large and Small Catechisms; daughter Magdalena born
1531	Son Martin born
1533	Son Paul born; named after the apostle whose writings brought such comfort to both his parents
1534	Luther publishes German translation of the complete Bible
1534	Daughter Margarethe born
1534	Henry VIII breaks from Rome, establishing the Church of England

1542 Magdalena (age 13) dies

1543 Copernicus publishes document announcing sun is center of universe

1546 Luther (age 62) dies of natural causes in Eisleben (February 18); buried in front of the pulpit in the Castle Church in Wittenberg